FRANCIS FRITH'S

NORFOLK VILLAGES

PHOTOGRAPHIC MEMORIES

Elizabeth Purdy was born in Northumberland and educated at Harrogate Ladies' College and Edinburgh University. While working as an Administrative Officer in the Colonial Service in Northern Nigeria she met and married John Purdy, a Norfolkman. In 1963, following Nigerian independence, they returned to Norfolk where Elizabeth enjoyed a very busy and full life as wife and mother, active in the local community. Her involvement with the WI gave her the opportunity to visit remote corners of Norfolk and to develop her love of rural life. Now widowed, Elizabeth has two sons, a daughter and five lovely grandchildren.

FRANCIS FRITH'S
PHOTOGRAPHIC MEMORIES

PHOTOGRAPHIC MEMORIES

NORFOLK VILLAGES

ELIZABETH PURDY

First published in the United Kingdom in 2003 by
Frith Book Company Ltd

Hardback Edition 2003
ISBN 1-85937-649-5

British Library Cataloguing in Publication Data

Francis Frith's - Norfolk Villages
Elizabeth Purdy

Frith Book Company Ltd
Frith's Barn, Teffont,
Salisbury, Wiltshire SP3 5QP
Tel: +44 (0) 1722 716 376
Email: info@francisfrith.co.uk
www.francisfrith.co.uk

Printed and bound in Great Britain

Front Cover: **HAPPISBURGH**, *The Village c1965* H304085
Frontispiece: **HOVETON**, *The Village 1921* 70890

The colour-tinting is for illustrative purposes only, and is not intended to be historically accurate

AS WITH ANY HISTORICAL DATABASE THE FRITH ARCHIVE IS CONSTANTLY BEING CORRECTED AND IMPROVED AND THE PUBLISHERS WOULD WELCOME INFORMATION ON OMISSIONS OR INACCURACIES

CONTENTS

FRANCIS FRITH
VICTORIAN PIONEER

FRANCIS FRITH, founder of the world-famous photographic archive, was a complex and multi-talented man. A devout Quaker and a highly successful Victorian businessman, he was philosophic by nature and pioneering in outlook.

By 1855 he had already established a wholesale grocery business in Liverpool, and sold it for the astonishing sum of £200,000, which is the equivalent today of over £15,000,000. Now a very rich man, he was able to indulge his passion for travel. As a child he had pored over travel books written by early explorers, and his fancy and imagination had been stirred by family holidays to the sublime mountain regions of Wales and Scotland. 'What lands of spirit-stirring and enriching scenes and places!' he had written. He was to return to these scenes of grandeur in later years to 'recapture the thousands of vivid and tender memories', but with a different purpose. Now in his thirties, and captivated by the new science of photography, Frith set out on a series of pioneering journeys up the Nile and to the Near East that occupied him from 1856 until 1860.

INTRIGUE AND EXPLORATION

These far-flung journeys were packed with intrigue and adventure. In his life story, written when he was sixty-three, Frith tells of being held captive by bandits, and of fighting 'an awful midnight battle to the very point of surrender with a deadly pack of hungry, wild dogs'. Wearing flowing Arab costume, Frith arrived at Akaba by camel seventy years before Lawrence of Arabia, where he encountered 'desert princes and rival sheikhs, blazing with jewel-hilted swords'.

He was the first photographer to venture beyond the sixth cataract of the Nile. Africa was still the mysterious 'Dark Continent', and Stanley and Livingstone's historic meeting was a decade into the future. The conditions for picture taking confound belief. He laboured for hours in his wicker dark-room in the sweltering heat of the desert, while the volatile chemicals fizzed dangerously in their trays. Back in London he exhibited his photographs and was 'rapturously cheered' by members of the Royal Society. His reputation as a photographer was made overnight.

VENTURE OF A LIFE-TIME

Characteristically, Frith quickly spotted the opportunity to create a new business as a specialist publisher of photographs. He lived in an era of immense and sometimes violent change.

For the poor in the early part of Victoria's reign work was exhausting and the hours long, and people had precious little free time to enjoy themselves. Most had no transport other than a cart or gig at their disposal, and rarely travelled far beyond the boundaries of their own town or village. However, by the 1870s the railways had threaded their way across the country, and Bank Holidays and half-day Saturdays had been made obligatory by Act of Parliament. All of a sudden the working man and his family were able to enjoy days out and see a little more of the world.

With typical business acumen, Francis Frith foresaw that these new tourists would enjoy having souvenirs to commemorate their days out. In 1860 he married Mary Ann Rosling and set out on a new career: his aim was to photograph every city, town and village in Britain. For the next thirty years he travelled the country by train and by pony and trap, producing fine photographs of seaside resorts and beauty spots that were keenly bought by millions of Victorians. These prints were painstakingly pasted into family albums and pored over during the dark nights of winter, rekindling precious memories of summer excursions.

THE RISE OF FRITH & CO

Frith's studio was soon supplying retail shops all over the country. To meet the demand he gathered about him a small team of photographers, and published the work of independent artist-photographers of the calibre of Roger Fenton and Francis Bedford. In order to gain some understanding of the scale of Frith's business one only has to look at the catalogue issued by Frith & Co in 1886: it runs to some 670 pages, listing not only many thousands of views of the British Isles but also many photographs of most European countries, and China, Japan, the USA and Canada - note the sample page shown on page 9 from the hand-written Frith & Co ledgers recording the pictures. By 1890 Frith had created the greatest specialist photographic publishing company in the world, with over 2,000 sales outlets - more than the combined number that Boots and WH Smith have today! The picture on the next page shows the Frith & Co display board at Ingleton in the Yorkshire Dales (left of window). Beautifully constructed with a mahogany frame and gilt inserts, it could display up to a dozen local scenes.

POSTCARD BONANZA

The ever-popular holiday postcard we know today took many years to develop. In 1870 the Post Office issued the first plain cards, with a pre-printed stamp on one face. In 1894 they allowed other publishers' cards to be sent through the mail with an attached adhesive halfpenny stamp. Demand grew rapidly, and in 1895 a new size of postcard was permitted called the court card, but there was little room for illustration. In 1899, a year after Frith's death, a new card measuring 5.5 x 3.5 inches became the standard format, but it was not until 1902 that the divided back came into being, so that the address and message could be on one face and a full-size illustration on the other. Frith & Co were in the vanguard of postcard development: Frith's sons Eustace and Cyril continued their father's monumental task, expanding the number of views offered to the public and recording more and more places in

5	... College, View from the ...		+		
6	St Catherine's College	+			
7	Senate House & Library	+			
8			+		
9	Gerrard Hostel Bridge	+	+	+	+
30	Geological Museum		+		
1	Addenbrooke's Hospital		+		
2	St Mary's Church		+		
3	Fitzwilliam Museum, Pitt Press &c		+		
4			+		
5	Buxton, The Crescent			+	
6	" The Colonnade			+	
7	" Public Gardens			+	
8				+	
9	Haddon Hall, View from the Terrace			+	
40	Millers Dale			+	

Britain, as the coasts and countryside were opened up to mass travel.

Francis Frith had died in 1898 at his villa in Cannes, his great project still growing. The archive he created continued in business for another seventy years. By 1970 it contained over a third of a million pictures showing 7,000 British towns and villages.

FRANCIS FRITH'S LEGACY

Frith's legacy to us today is of immense significance and value, for the magnificent archive of evocative photographs he created provides a unique record of change in the cities, towns and villages throughout Britain over a century and more. Frith and his fellow studio photographers revisited locations many times down the years to update their views, compiling for us an enthralling and colourful pageant of British life and character.

We are fortunate that Frith was dedicated to recording the minutiae of everyday life. For it is this sheer wealth of visual data, the painstaking chronicle of changes in dress, transport, street layouts, buildings, housing, engineering and landscape that captivates us so much today. His remarkable images offer us a powerful link with the past and with the lives of our ancestors.

THE VALUE OF THE ARCHIVE TODAY

Computers have now made it possible for Frith's many thousands of images to be accessed almost instantly. Frith's images are increasingly used as visual resources, by social historians, by researchers into genealogy and ancestry, by architects and town planners, and by teachers involved in local history projects.

In addition, the archive offers every one of us an opportunity to examine the places where we and our families have lived and worked down the years. Highly successful in Frith's own era, the archive is now, a century and more on, entering a new phase of popularity. Historians consider the Francis Frith Collection to be of prime national importance. It is the only archive of its kind remaining in private ownership. Francis Frith's archive is now housed in an historic timber barn in the beautiful village of Teffont in Wiltshire. Its founder would not recognize the archive office as it is today. In place of the many thousands of dusty boxes containing glass plate negatives and an all-pervading odour of photographic chemicals, there are now ranks of computer screens. He would be amazed to watch his images travelling round the world at unimaginable speeds through internet lines.

The archive's future is both bright and exciting. Francis Frith, with his unshakeable belief in making photographs available to the greatest number of people, would undoubtedly approve of what is being done today with his lifetime's work. His photographs depicting our shared past are now bringing pleasure and enlightenment to millions around the world a century and more after his death.

NORFOLK
AN INTRODUCTION

TURN off the A1 or the M11, and out to the east there is a county like no other.

It has a wealth of interest, and a great deal of beauty. Until the 15th century, Norwich was second only to London in size and importance. It was the gateway to Europe for the exchange of goods and ideas before America was discovered and trade turned westwards. With the growing power of the European Union, perhaps the time is coming when Norfolk will again become an area of strategic importance.

Now is the time to discover the real Norfolk, the delightful rural country it has become, before this gentle backwater is overpowered by the rush and aggression of the modern world. When we look at these interesting photographs taken more than fifty years ago, we realize that many changes have already taken place.

Norfolk is almost an island: two sides are bordered by the North Sea, while the western

BELAUGH, *The Village from the River c1955* B495005

boundary runs virtually beside the River Great Ouse, which flows into the Wash at Kings Lynn. Only a few yards from the Ouse is the source of the Waveney, which flows eastward, forming the boundary with Suffolk and coming out into the North Sea at Great Yarmouth.

The west of Norfolk south of King's Lynn is fenland, and the marshes were virtually impassable before the Romans began to drain them. The dykes fell into disrepair when the Roman legions departed in the 5th century; Norfolk again became isolated until 18th-century engineers initiated a massive system of drains and sluices, which nowadays controls the flow of water as far as the midlands and the London area. At Denver sluice it is possible to see this intricate system which manipulates a mighty force of water.

Perhaps its geography has contributed to, if not caused, the isolationist character of the Norfolkman. 'We do different,' say Norfolk people. Indeed, they are an independent-minded people. They are said to be unfriendly, but that does them an injustice. They are naturally reserved, and suspicious of 'furriners', but friendly enough, and even welcoming, if the incomer is prepared to accept Norfolk and its people as they are, rather than wanting to sweep away all the familiar cobwebs and replace them with untrusted new ways.

Even the Romans found it difficult to maintain order among the native tribes. The pillaging and outrages committed by the Romans so incensed the Iceni that their queen, Boudicca, led a well-documented uprising. The Roman camp and town at Colchester were destroyed, and the insurgents sacked London before they were finally defeated on the spot now known as King's Cross. The death of Boudicca herself marked the virtual end of powerful tribal insurrection in East Anglia. The Romans left the foundations of a road system, and there is plentiful evidence of their occupation, particularly around their military stations at Brancaster, on the north coast, Caistor (near Yarmouth), Caistor (near Norwich), Tasburgh and Thetford. Bricks, pottery, and coins are relatively common finds in the fields of Norfolk, and stones from former Roman buildings often appear in later constructions.

Germanic tribes from Saxony and then Denmark came in waves, seizing the land, making settlements and imposing their own social structures. The history of many Norfolk villages can be traced back to this period, long before the Norman conquest. Aylsham, for instance, owes its name to a Saxon thegn, Aegel, who established his homestead there about AD 500.

Except for the small, brown carrstone found occasionally near King's Lynn, flint is the only stone naturally found in Norfolk. Consequently its early buildings (other than the church and possibly a fortified house for the thegn) were built of wood and have not survived. The stone to build Norwich Cathedral in 1094 was brought from Caen in Normandy by sea and up the River Wensum to a site close by its landing-place. But there are many churches which can trace their foundation well before 1066. Their distinguishing feature is usually a round, flint tower, of which 119 survive in Norfolk, more than the total elsewhere. Although the church was the centre of the community, there are many instances of present-day villages being at some distance from their church. It is thought that at the time of the Black Death in the 14th century, the villagers moved for health reasons to new houses away from the area of infection.

A local curiosity hereabouts is shared churchyards. Two churches, occasionally three, usually Saxon in origin, were built within yards of each other. This probably resulted from groups of monks living in adjacent communities each wanting their own place of worship. The land around would belong to different thegns, to whom villagers looked for their livelihood and in whose neighbourhood, away from the church, they lived and worked and sought justice.

Sir John Betjeman regarded Norfolk as one of the greatest art treasures of Europe on account of its medieval country churches. There are well over 700 churches here, a gem in nearly every village. No two are alike, and they all reflect the love and devotion of centuries in their additions and furnishings. Now many tiny villages struggle to keep their church repaired and open: 20% of the population of Norfolk lives in a parish of under 1000 people, and 20% of those are communities of fewer than 300.

Villages have grown out of settlements wherever a living could be made, and are usually sited on locally high ground and near water. Many have developed along a droving lane which has become a main highway. These linear villages,

BLAKENEY, *The Quay, Looking East c1955* B121038

such as Long Stratton, Horsford, and Watton, usually have a wide main street, a relic of the days when cattle and sheep were driven through.

More common, and perhaps more picturesque, are villages centred round a green, often with a pond or a stream running through. Burnham Market, Hingham, Great Massingham, and Brooke are examples. There are also a number of estate villages in Norfolk, built by large landowners to house their employees and pensioners. Such are Glandford, Houghton, and Wolferton, identifiable by the uniformity of the buildings. Often a river divides two villages on opposite banks: Loddon and Chedgrave, Corpusty and Saxthorpe, Wroxham and Hoveton, for instance.

Over the last 100 years life in a rural village has changed almost out of recognition. Most villages now have piped water to each house. The old village pumps, so generously donated by local benefactors, are now redundant, picturesque reminders of days when water was drawn by hand and carried in a bucket. Many villages have sewage pipes laid. The night soil collector has gone, and even the cesspit tanker is a rare sight. Overhead electricity and telephone supplies are universal, though subject to interference in stormy weather. Nevertheless, a surprising number of properties (including my own, only two miles out of the town), depend on well water or a bore hole and deal with their own sewage.

A century ago every village had its own primary school - a light, airy, purpose built building with outside lavatories and a large playground. The children who were sufficiently academic proceeded at eleven to a town grammar school, such as the Paston School at North Walsham, where Horatio Nelson was a boarder. As education became more sophisticated in its curriculum, and demographic changes reduced the number of children in villages, these small schools were closed and the children were bussed to larger schools in nearby towns. This movement has had a deleterious effect on village life, as the children now look to another community for their friends and entertainment.

During the first part of the 20th century, many village halls were built. They ranged from the basic, four wooden walls and a tin roof, to solid brick and tiles, complete with kitchen, toilets and a stage, on which many a budding actress lisped her first lines in front of a sympathetic audience of parents and neighbours. Two thirds of the villages in Norfolk had a Women's Institute, providing education and community service, while their menfolk supported the village pub. Parish Council meetings, bingo, wedding receptions and more, all made use of the village hall. By the 1980s a plethora of health and safety regulations meant that many halls had reached the end of their useful life. However, grants from Millennium and Lottery funds, matched by similar sums raised in the village, have enabled many halls to be rebuilt as modern community centres, keeping alive the social life of the village.

In most small villages the shop and post office have closed - town supermarkets provide more variety at cheaper prices, and working women find them more convenient. Many pubs have closed, as television provides entertainment at home. Those bus services which remain are infrequent. Doctors no longer have an out-of-town surgery. A private car is no longer a luxury; even two cars per household are a necessity in many cases. Rural life has become very difficult for those who are unable to drive.

Norfolk's prime industry is agriculture. The rich, black earth of the fens and the lighter, sandy soil further east produce heavy crops of corn, sugar beet, potatoes, and kale for animal feed. Reeds, which abound in the Broads area and along other river banks, are cultivated and harvested to make a very high quality thatching material. The use of increasingly large and more efficient machinery has, however, reduced employment opportunities in agriculture. Sheep are still bred, but the woollen industry, whose wealth built so many glorious churches and where the village of Worsted gave its name to fine cloth, has moved elsewhere.

Fishing, which once played such an important part in the Norfolk economy, has declined dramatically since the 1970s when regulations and quotas virtually strangled the industry. The herring fleet of Yarmouth is no more. A little offshore fishing continues, and it is still possible to buy the famous Cromer crabs.

Although traditional industries have declined, others have replaced them. The largest of these new employers is tourism, for Norfolk has so much to offer the visitor. For those interested in history there are more than ten thousand listed buildings, and many fine mansions are open to the public. The National Trust has four major properties, as well as numerous smaller sites. Public footpaths are clearly signposted and are very well maintained, varying in length and difficulty.

There are 200 conservation areas in the county, which provide wonderful opportunities to enjoy wildlife and views. The Norfolk Naturalist Trust was the first voluntary group in the country to act to preserve species of wildlife, many of which are unique to the area, and it has been a blueprint for other counties. Artists find inspiration in the clear light and fantastic cloud formations afforded by the low horizons of the north coast and the marshlands, while naturalists and birdwatchers discover a wealth of interest.

The Broads, covering 303 square kilometres, now has the status of a National Park and is, perhaps, the best known part of Norfolk. With 250 miles of waterways, opportunities for sailing or exploring by motor cruiser are enormous; this has brought about the expansion of the boat building industry, and the development of tourist attractions.

Farmers have not been slow to seize opportunities for diversification. Old farm buildings, now redundant, make picturesque homes, and many barns have been sympathetically converted to holiday accommodation. Craft workshops, art galleries, and offices are now to be found in rustic locations. Builders, caretakers, and cleaners have all found plenty of employment opportunities.

While many may regret the changes that are taking place, the North Folk are adapting and developing as they have always done over the centuries since their Saxon forbears arrived. Many hundreds of new homes are being built in villages throughout Norfolk. The new inhabitants, often retired, bring fresh life to small communities, and learn to love, as many of us already have, the glorious natural beauty of wide open spaces, magnificent sunsets and the abundance of wildlife.

THE EAST COAST

Each year the force of the North Sea tides and strong currents erode a fraction more of the Norfolk coast, leaving behind a long stretch of golden sand extending from Cromer down to Great Yarmouth. Occasional cliffs give a vantage point on which to place a church, but generally the countryside is flat, agricultural land, exposed to the chill winds from the North Pole and the east wind from the Ural mountains.

OVERSTRAND, *The Post Office 1921* 71002

The long main street of this little residential town remains much as it was in 1921. The post office has moved from the corner to the building with bay windows on the first floor, formerly Stafford House Tea Rooms (centre). The house agency (left) is now the Singing Kettle.

OVERSTRAND
The Churches 1922
72660

This is a mystery picture. There is now no trace whatsoever of the church on the left. Was it a chapel belonging to the Hall behind the churchyard? St Martin's church, with its square tower, is constructed of local flints. It has a striking, modern east window depicting St Cuthbert and St Martin, and a war memorial given by the sisters of those killed in the Great War.

TRIMINGHAM, *Loop Road c1955* T226012

These attractive buildings, one built of local flints, the other of rendered brick with a wood-faced gable (unusual in Norfolk), which housed the post office, are now derelict. The sea has eroded the cliff, and immediately beyond the buildings there is a sheer drop. The road is no more.

TRIMINGHAM
The Crown and Anchor c1955
T226013

In its heyday this must have been a smart hotel for seaside visitors. Advertising vacancies for full board and dinner/bed & breakfast, the outside of the hotel requires redecoration, although an elaborate wrought iron sign and a television aerial indicate some effort to keep up to date. Alas, it was burnt down many years ago.

PASTON, *The Old Mill c1965* P248001

Known as Stow Mill, this four-storey, brick-built tower, tarred for weatherproofing, was a working windmill, grinding corn from 1827 until the 1930s, when it became a private house. It is unusual in that it was designed with dummy windows on the upper floors so as to be scenically attractive. Its preservation began in 1960 when four new sails and a skeleton fantail were fitted. In 1980 further repairs enabled the cap to turn to face the biting wind once again. It is now open to the public.

▼ **PASTON,** *The Tithe Barn c1965* P248012

This scheduled monument is also known as Paston Great Barn. It has two huge doorways and a magnificent thatched roof. Since this photograph was taken the greenhouse has been removed, and the annexe in the centre front of the barn is being re-roofed.

► **BACTON**
The Abbey Gateway c1955 B493022

We are looking back from the abbey through the great gateway to the village, where a row of flint cottages can be seen on the right. These may once have been almshouses, but have now been modernised. The gateway itself has had the ivy removed, which should help to preserve it.

BACTON
The Abbey 1933
85860

The ruins of Bacton Abbey lie within the bounds of a private farm, and they are not now accessible to the public. The building in this photograph appears to be part of the chancel, whose pointed arches indicate that the building is 14th-century. It is sad to see such a potentially beautiful place overgrown with ivy and used as a dumping ground for old farm machinery.

BACTON
The Village c1955
B493070

This view from the end of the road sweeping up towards the abbey shows the main road before the cottage on the right was demolished. The left-hand house has a beautifully thatched roof, but its lower extension is now tiled. The protruding upper storey could indicate a basically timber-framed structure.

HAPPISBURGH
The Village c1965
H304085

The tall, slender tower of the church of St Mary the Virgin, perched on a small hill, affords stupendous views over the flat countryside and the magnificent sunsets to the west. The whitewashed cottage, with its characteristic Norfolk tiled roof and dormer window, nestles among chestnut trees. What are all the cars waiting for? Are the drivers in the little shop (left)?

► SEA PALLING
The Village c1955
S470078

This view from St Margaret's church shows clearly the low-lying nature of the countryside round this small seaside village. It was formerly a fishing and agricultural community, but now most workers commute to Yarmouth or Norwich for employment. Notice the productive fields right up to the edge of the cottage gardens, and the Nissen huts on the left, relics of the war.

◄ SEA PALLING
The Village c1950
S470005

In 1953 high tides caused the sea to sweep over the dunes and inundate the northern end of the village. Several houses were swept away, and seven people lost their lives. This photograph was taken before the flood; it shows The Lifeboat Inn (right), recalling the station operated by the RNLI from 1858 to 1931. An inflatable rescue boat is now manned by volunteers.

▲ **SEA PALLING,** *Beach Road c1955* S470014

Here we see a terrace of brick built cottages and a larger house which withstood the 1953 flood; they were probably built early in the 20th century. Telephones and electricity had arrived, but there are no TV aerials to be seen.

◄ **WINTERTON-ON-SEA** *The Fisherman's Return c1955* W357097

An attractive forecourt in front of the pub awaits thirsty fishermen. Very new houses have replaced the thatched cottages next door, but further along the Methodist chapel, built in 1876, still advertises its services and its coffee mornings.

WINTERTON-ON-SEA
King Street c1955
W357099

Carrying bucket and spade, a mother and her child trudge back from the beach at the end of the lane. Many of these cottages can still be identified, but the white-painted Cottage Café (centre) has been redeveloped.

HEMSBY
The Beach Approach c1955
H306002

This view shows a scene typical of a coastal holiday resort in the 1950s. At the end of the track to the beach were a snack bar and a temporary stall selling the popular sticky candy floss. Fashions of the day include baggy trousers and several cardigans.

SCRATBY, *The Bungalows c1955* S463035

It is surprising, perhaps, that many of these insubstantial little holiday homes are still looking out onto the cold North Sea nearly 50 years on. The gardens were only a patch of grass, separated from the neighbours by wire fences with concrete posts, and there were no garages for the cars which ventured along the potholed, muddy track along the cliff. The area in the distance is now covered with residential buildings.

SCRATBY
The Cliffs c1955
S463028

Boys of the 1950s indulged, as generations did before them, in watching ships far out to sea. The photograph shows the wide expanse of sandy beach which is typical of the east coast of Norfolk, while the buildings further along the cliff show that already holiday accommodation was encroaching on the natural environment.

ORMESBY
The Beach c1935
O78003

Now known as 'California', the beach at Ormesby is lovely golden sand. It is possible to see how pounding of the sea at high tides is causing erosion of the cliffs. Tents of the 1930s provided good shelter with their tall frames and canvas sides. Clothing was more formal then, though: two men are well covered by their fashionable bathing costumes, while the boy on the left is wearing a jacket and tie.

ORMESBY, *The Green c1955* O78017

The main road to Yarmouth now bypasses Ormesby St Margaret, which has returned to being a quiet village surrounding a lovely green. The Royal Oak Hotel on the left of the picture still welcomes visitors, but many of the old cottages have been replaced by new homes, and the road to the beach is lined by holiday chalets.

MARTHAM
The Green c1960
M228027

A few miles inland from the sea is the attractive village of Martham, with cottages and Georgian houses surrounding the peaceful village green. The tree on the left of the picture has gone, but goats still graze beneath the chestnut trees. Today the huge sails of an electricity-generating wind farm can be glimpsed behind the white cottage, and the thatched cottage is now a fish shop.

HOPTON, *The Village c1965* H310117

Midway between Yarmouth and Lowestoft lies the village of Hopton, where holiday and retirement bungalows abound. It is surprising, perhaps, that this general store, now Hopton Newsagents, is virtually unchanged since 1965. Postcards are still for sale outside, but Hopton-on-Sea Rock sells for more than the pre-decimalisation prices (from 3d to 2s) shown on the board on the step. The tower on the left is the principal remaining portion of St. Margaret's church.

COLTISHALL
The Village c1955 C417065

This photograph of the war memorial in the centre of the long, rather straggling village shows great chestnut trees, which have now been replaced by newly planted saplings. The shop front in the middle of the picture is now the Coltishall Pharmacy, and The Cabinetmakers Arms (right) is a private house known as The Cabinet. The petrol station on 'Coltishall Island' (straight ahead) has smartened up.

BROADLAND

THE geography of the low-lying land east of Norwich has changed considerably since Roman times, for the action of the North Sea is continually altering the coastline. From the 7th century to the 14th century this was one of the most heavily populated and prosperous parts of the country. Previously heavily wooded, the tree cover was stripped early on, and areas of peat were dug to provide alternative fuel. To facilitate transport of the peat, it was extracted near the rivers - the Bure with its tributaries the Ant and the Thurne, the Yare, and the Waveney. By the 13th century many of the peat pits had flooded and were abandoned. These pits and rivers now form the network of broads. The upper reaches of the rivers traverse gently wooded, agricultural countryside, with elder carr (marshy copses) and reeds softening the water's edge. Towards the south and east marshland predominates. Drainage mills can still be seen, enabling cattle to graze. It is a wildlife paradise. Trade went up the Bure as far as Aylsham until August 1912, when a tremendous rainfall destroyed all the locks above Coltishall, where boats now have to halt. Merchant boats traded up the Yare to Norwich as late as the 1980s.

COLTISHALL
A Cornfield 1902 48128

This delightful scene shows the lightly wooded, gently rolling nature of this agricultural area. The corn has been harvested, bundled and set in stooks to dry before being taken to be threshed. The little girls are wearing hats and pinafores over their dresses, and the boys have caps in the fashion of the day.

▼ **COLTISHALL,** *The Church c1955* C417023

The church of St John the Baptist, with its thatched nave, now boasts a clock on its tower. The house opposite (with an open window) has been demolished to make way for a car park for The Red Lion pub. Fred A Coman, Plumbers and Decorators (right) has departed, and his house, with its interesting Dutch gabled frontage, is now a private residence.

▶ **BELAUGH**
The Staithe 1934 86395

A tranquil reach of the river Bure reflects almost the whole of the tiny village of Belaugh, which is hidden in a loop off the road from Coltishall to Wroxham. The staithe in the centre of the picture provides mooring for pleasure craft. It has been tidied, but remains unspoiled.

COLTISHALL
On the Banks of the Bure 1902
48173

The thatcher's craft is one of the staple industries of broads villages. This photograph illustrates reeds growing at the edge of a broad, with the cut stalks stacked by the cottage. The shallow-bottomed boat on the right is used for transporting the reeds, and finished thatch can be seen on the roof of the cottage and outhouses.

BELAUGH
The Church c1955
B495159

This lovely village church, dedicated to St Peter, has a fine rood screen depicting the twelve apostles. Their faces have been obliterated by, it is said, a zealous Puritan during the Civil War. The tiny churchyard is a designated conservation area, with particularly interesting ferns and lichens.

WROXHAM
The Yacht Yard c1940 W156110

Many of the old, individual boatyards have been absorbed by larger firms, but Wroxham remains one of the principal boat building and hiring villages in broadland. Although sailing boats are still seen on the broads, they are now vastly outnumbered by motor cruisers. Were Fred and Alfred the sons mentioned on Ernest Collins' board (right)?

WROXHAM, *The Bridge c1940* W156120

The river Bure divides the mainly residential area of Wroxham to the west and the village of Hoveton on the east side of the bridge. In the 1960s this old stone and brick bridge was deemed unsafe for heavy traffic and a 'temporary' bridge was superimposed. Later a footbridge was added to the south, which in turn was replaced by a more permanent structure in 2002.

HOVETON

The Village 1934 86354

Known as 'Roys of Wroxham', this village shop occupies the heart of Hoveton and once claimed to be the largest village shop in the world. The buildings are much the same today, but the amount of traffic is vastly different, being controlled by roundabouts, traffic lights and pedestrian crossings. The Walls ice cream seller with his tricycle next to the vending machine (left) was typical of the 1930s.

HOVETON, *The Village c1955* H399137

It is twenty years after No 86354, and the semi-circular fascia of Roys grocery department has been redecorated. The buildings on the left were redeveloped in the 1970s, and again reconstructed after being destroyed by fire in 1996. Notice the old wire litter bin by the sign post, and the petrol pump behind the parked cars (centre).

ERY
SONS.
CLINCHER
TYRES

HOVETON
The Village 1921 70890

We are looking towards the bridge that leads over the Bure to Wroxham. The buildings in the foreground can be recognised today by their interesting roof lines, although Wards Telegraphic Stores is now an estate agent and Roys Millinery on the left is now the toy department. It is hard to imagine the hand carts selling fruit and vegetables on the present main road to Norwich with its never-ending stream of traffic.

STALHAM
High Street c1955
S467068

A solitary car, but at least five bicycles, in the main street contrast with the busy traffic today. Most of the buildings are still identifiable, albeit selling different goods. The Swan Hotel (behind the car) still offers refreshment. The pavement is in need of repair, and litter was an eyesore even in 1955.

STALHAM
The Village 1952
S467067

Just off the High Street is St John's Road, a quiet, residential street of semi-detached brick houses, each with a small garden and neatly trimmed hedge. There are no television aerials and no garages.

▲ **HICKLING,** *The Pleasure Boat Inn c1955* H307012

Alongside the staithe a short distance from Hickling Broad, we find the Pleasure Boat Inn, a popular mooring place for water-borne visitors. The sailing boat, two motor cruisers and the dinghy all have wooden hulls; only the motor launch might be constructed of modern fibreglass. What are the people on the sailing boat (right) examining with such care?

◄ **LUDHAM**
The View from the Church Tower c1935
L110013

Ludham village is set in rich agricultural land. This photograph was taken before many hedges were grubbed out in the 1950s and 60s. The village itself has grown up alongside the road from Wroxham towards Great Yarmouth. The war memorial at the corner of the churchyard commemorates the dead of two World Wars. The vehicle outside the kissing gate at the end of the path (left) is a 1920s model.

LUDHAM
The River Ant and the Mill c1955 L110057

The 20 feet high tower windmill, which stood on the west bank of the River Ant, was used to pump water to drain the marshland. It fell into disrepair when electricity became the source of power, and now no trace of it remains.

◄ **LUDHAM**
The Village c1955 L110073

The centre of the village spans the main road, so that even with little traffic it seems a strange place for a group of men to stand. On the right the garage with the petrol hand pump displays an early Automobile Association badge. Next to it is The King's Arms. Across the road is the post office and grocery store, which has now become Barnaby's Bistro.

▲ **POTTER HEIGHAM,** *Riverside Bungalows c1955* P167029

Tall masts, square sails and broad, shallow hulls identify these two craft as wherries, boats characteristic of broadland, which were used for transporting goods up country from the port at Yarmouth. Only a few remain today as curiosities for tourists. The bungalows are typical of holiday homes, with boatshed and moorings giving access to the river and broads.

◄ **POTTER HEIGHAM**
The Bridge c1955
P167062

Lights regulated the traffic crossing the bridge before a bypass was built in the 1970s. A notice over the round central arch warns boats to 'Go slow, sound horn, lower canopy.' The mast of the wherry has been lowered to pass under the bridge, and the boatman is 'quanting', ie propelling the boat with a pole. Broad Haven boatyard on the left and the refuelling station on the right indicate the importance of Potter Heigham in the boat industry.

NO PARKING PLEASE
BUS STOP

HORNING
The Village c1965
H116144

The Swan Hotel, on the left of the photograph, backs on to the Bure. The building at the end has given way to an official car park. Roys, on the right, has become Horning Stores, but the building retains its unusual, attractive brick pediment. The lady with a moped outside Roys is wearing a crash helmet, not often seen in 1965.

► HORNING
Lower Street c1965 H116119

Running alongside the Bure, Horning is a popular small holiday village. New houses have replaced Percival's engineering workshop (centre); Geraldine Barber (left) has closed, and the whole property is derelict. But the white-painted houses further down the street, one dated 1682, remain.

◄ RANWORTH
The Staithe 1934
86388

Here we have a glimpse of Ranworth Broad with sailing boats and motor cruisers. The thatched building on the right is now a café and gift shop, but the Maltsters Inn on the left is little changed. Ranworth is a charming little village, and there is a magnificent view over broadland from the top of the church tower.

▲ **STOKESBY,** *The Post Office c1965* S469044

A hidden gem beside the river Bure, Stokesby has a charming green beside which boats can pause on their way up to the northern broads. Although the Post Office Stores has become a candle workshop and tearoom with a garden, the village still has its own post office further along the street.

◄ **CANTLEY**
The Red House Hotel c1965 C414006

154 years ago, when navvies were building the Norwich to Yarmouth railway, a hostel was built beside the river Yare. It was enlarged to become a public house in about 1895, and is now a watering hole popular both with holidaymakers and with workers from the sugar beet factory next door. From December to March lorries piled high with beet rumble down the country lanes, bringing the harvest to be processed into sugar.

▼ **REEDHAM,** *The Ferry Inn c1955* R303057

A ferry at Reedham is the only means for pedestrian or motor traffic to cross the River Yare for the 25 miles of its course between Norwich and Yarmouth. The lovely chestnut tree in front of the Ferry Inn has given way to a restaurant extension, and the clock on the right of the inn's facade, so useful for ferry travellers, has disappeared also.

► **REEDHAM**
The Lord Nelson c1955
R303066

Named after Norfolk's most popular hero, the Lord Nelson stands beside the waterfront looking across the windswept Halvergate marshes with their abundant wildlife. It is an attractive building, now incorporating the former garage, with stonework decoration unusual in Norfolk villages. The cottage on the left is now the village post office.

◄ **REEDHAM**
The Ship Hotel c1955 R303040

This is yet another delightful hostelry beside the river for visitors to Reedham. The thatched cottage on the left of the photograph was formerly another public house, the Brickworkers Arms, before it became a tearooms and subsequently a private house.

► **REEDHAM**
The Bridge c1955
R303039

The railway from Norwich to Lowestoft crosses the Yare via this swing bridge at Reedham. The river here is tidal, and although most commercial traffic now goes by road, a few large ships still go as far as Norwich. Much work is currently (2003) in progress to strengthen flood defences along the river bank.

BRUNDALL, *The River c1955* B497016

The alder carr fringing the river in this scene is typical of that found alongside the upper reaches of the Bure and its tributaries, the Ant and the Thurne. The sailing boat with its broad-based, wooden hull would more likely be a fibreglass motorised cruiser today – and today one would certainly not find someone smoking beside a petrol dump!

NORTH NORFOLK

BETWEEN the north coast and Norwich lies a stretch of rich agricultural land with small market towns spaced roughly twelve miles apart, enabling farmers of former times to walk from their village to market and back in one day. It is gently rolling, wooded countryside reflecting a life far removed from the bustling metropolis.

WORSTEAD, *St Mary's Church c1955* W355009

This magnificent flint church was built in the heyday of the wool trade. For over forty years an annual festival to raise funds for its restoration has been held in this tiny village which gave its name to fine woollen cloth. The church has many noteworthy features, including a finely carved roodscreen, a tall font cover and a striking modern tapestry in wool depicting the baptism of Christ.

◄ **THORPE MARKET**
Pitt Cottage c1955
T256015

On the North Walsham road, on the outskirts of this small, scattered village, stands this typical example of a Norfolk farmhouse, constructed of flint and thatch, with casement windows and a thatched porch over the door. John Notley's Jersey cows are no longer there, nor is it now permitted for cream to be sold at the roadside.

◄ **THORPE MARKET** *The Post Office c1955* T256014

Here we see two examples of a row of cottages, Norfolk style – both basically single-storey with dormer windows in the roof. One row (left) is built of local bricks and has a tiled roof, while the other (in the distance) is constructed of flints and is thatched. The green between them now has a village sign commemorating the Queen's Silver Jubilee in 1977. The post office, the right-hand brick cottage, is now Poppyland Cottage.

▲ **ALDBOROUGH,** *The Green c1955* A278006

An annual fair has been held on the green in the middle of the village since its charter was granted by King John. Cricket and football in their seasons, horse trading and stock fairs all take place here. The white-painted cycle shop has become a private house, but The Black Boys to the left still offers refreshment. Further round, John Brown's house has had its white roof fascia removed.

◄ **ALDBOROUGH** *Thwaite Hill c1955* A278011

Beside the road stands a row of cottages, built over many years. There is now a newer one between the white-painted Georgian one and the 1930s one on the left. Along the lane a gentle rise, which here merits the title of hill, leads up between an avenue of oak trees towards Thwaite church.

THWAITE
The Church c1955
A278014

It is said that the Saxon tower of this tiny, simple church of All Saints was built in response to the rule of King Athelstan, who in AD 937 required every thegn to build a bell tower on his land. The nave is also 10th-century, and the south aisle was added in the 15th century.

CAWSTON, *The Village c1955* C415009

The old tree in the centre of the picture still stands today beside the tiled shed, but new houses have been built opposite. Mr Riley's grocery shop (straight ahead) has changed hands, and the garage with an early petrol pump outside has withdrawn from the roadside. What is the wire looped across the left hand house? Electricity? Telephone? Bell pull?

CAWSTON
New Street c1965
C415004

Nestling in the shade of St Agnes' church, this row of small bungalows was built in the 1960s, intended mainly for elderly residents. A popular Morris Minor car is parked in the street, but the houses have no garages. The somewhat stark appearance of the church tower belies the many lovely features to be discovered inside, including the porch, stained glass and misericords.

REEPHAM, *The View from the Church c1965* R304008

An open market place, surrounded by mainly 18th-century buildings, creates an attractive heart to the busy village. Many individual shops supply most of the needs of inhabitants – a pharmacy at the head of the street leading from the church, a butcher in the next building with a stepped gable, and HSBC bank next door. Riches grocery store is on the left, next to a wine merchant. Sun blinds conceal other shop fronts.

REEPHAM, *The Market Place c1965* R304022

Here we view the market place at ground level, facing towards the church. The Bircham Centre, whose rear view is centre left of photograph R304008 (page 55), stands on the far side behind the bus shelter. It houses a small library and many useful meeting rooms. To the right is The King's Arms, but the pub in the foreground is now shops. Individual shop fronts give character to the buildings.

REEPHAM
The Two Churches c1965 R304004

Reepham churchyard is most unusual in housing two complete churches and the ruins of a third. All are of Saxon origin. Three parishes, Reepham, Hackford and Whitwell converge at this point, and here a market developed. All Saints, Hackford, was burnt down in 1543, but Reepham St Mary (now used as the main church)and Whitwell St Michael (deconsecrated and used as a hall) have been physically joined.

MELTON CONSTABLE, *The School and the War Memorial 1922* 72619

The Victorian village school, light and airy, ceased to be used in the 1970s, when larger premises were built across the road. Boys and girls had separate entrances and playgrounds. The war memorial stone was very new in 1922, and wreaths were still being laid to the nineteen men who died in the First World War.

EAST BARSHAM
Sheep on the Fakenham Road 1929
82041

An open-roofed car waits patiently outside The White Horse Inn while the shepherd guides his flock up the road towards the tiny village. They are about to pass East Barsham Manor, a gloomy, Gothic house which is said to be haunted.

▼ **WALSINGHAM,** *The Sanctuary of Our Lady c1965* W13059

A devout noblewoman, Richeldis, had a vision of the Virgin Mary, who told her to copy her own home in Nazareth. A well on the site came to have healing properties, and Richeldis' son endowed 'England's Nazareth'. The shrine was founded in 1061, destroyed in 1538 and restored in 1922. Since then it has become a place of peace to many pilgrims worshipping there.

► **WALSINGHAM**
The Abbey, Knights Bridge 1926 79303

The ruined abbey stands in the beautiful grounds of a Georgian house. At snowdrop time, and when the daffodils are flowering, the grounds are often opened for the public to enjoy. This charming old bridge among the trees gazes at its reflection in the stream.

◄ **WALSINGHAM**
The Pump and Old Houses 1929 82032

This is an often-photographed corner of old Walsingham, showing the former pump from which the villagers used to obtain their water. The picturesque, timber-framed house opposite is probably 15th-century. The protruding upper storey of the shop on the right indicates that it is probably also a timber-framed building.

► **NORTH CREAKE**
Main Road c1955
N138013

This rather dull approach to an attractive small village has changed little. The Victoria public house closed in the 1970s and is now privately owned. Opposite, in the far, low-roofed building, is the smithy, which also doubles as the post office.

GREAT BIRCHAM, *The Village Sign c1965* G190036

The village sign, topped with the royal crest, illustrates Peddars Way, a prehistoric trading path, which runs close by. It was presented to Her Majesty the Queen by Bircham Girl Guides and Boy Scouts in 1960. Children are standing by the railings of the old school (right), built in 1860 by the Marquis of Cholmondley of nearby Houghton Hall to provide primary education for children of the three Birchams. He even clothed the children each year at his own expense.

GREAT MASSINGHAM *The Village Pond c1965* G210002

This photograph does not do justice to a beautiful village, which has two large, well-kept greens surrounded by Georgian houses. There is another pond beyond the hut in the centre of the photograph. Ducks, swans and geese are all to be seen enjoying the water.

GREAT MASSINGHAM, *The Swan and the Church c1965* G210015

The Swan, with its beautifully painted sign and the banner showing the barley emblem of Steward and Patterson, the brewers, is a public house no longer, but is being renovated for private habitation. St Mary's church, beyond the village shop in the white house, has very fine windows.

THE NORTH COAST

FROM Cromer on the north-east corner of Norfolk to Brancaster in the west, the coast is one of the most attractive areas of the county. Wide stretches of sandy beach lie sometimes beyond salt marshes, sometimes below cliffs with creeks leading to ancient harbours. At Brancaster there is a popular golf course among the dunes, the clubhouse cut off at high tide. Eastwards, at Holkham, there are enormous stretches of beach with the sea half a mile and more away at low tide. Flat salt marshes from Morston to Sheringham keep villages away from the shoreline, while at Weybourne the high cliffs afford some of the deepest approaches to land anywhere round the English coast. Along the whole stretch there is a long, low horizon providing wonderfully clear light, greatly appreciated by artists.

WEST RUNTON, *The Village c1955* W70008

A group of women mardle (Norfolk for 'gossip') outside a variety of shops, most of which still serve residents and the many visitors who come in the summer. Another lady enjoys a rest on a thoughtfully provided seat. The baker is now the Cat's Whiskers, and The Village Inn is a petrol station.

WEST RUNTON
The Village c1955
W70061

We are looking back from the opposite end of the street we saw in photograph No W70008. Most of the shops are the same, but the telephone kiosk has been moved to (or from?) a spot close to the signpost. Lloyds Bank and Barclays Bank were housed in very simple and apparently insecure buildings, and the petrol station then did not have to fulfil the stringent safety requirements of today.

BEESTON REGIS, *The Camping Site c1955* B538003

Exposed to the bitter north wind, All Saints' church stands on a mound overlooking a camp site (now a mobile home park) towards the sea. Inside is a lovely, delicate screen, complete with rood and 15th-century paintings.

▼ BEESTON REGIS, *Lodge Corner 1933* 85809

This is a typical Norfolk cottage built of flint, the only stone found locally, with brick corner supports. The decorative arched brick window frames, the tiled roof and gable windows with casements are features found throughout Norfolk. Avenues of beech trees are frequently to be seen in this area.

▶ WEYBOURNE

The Village c1955

W353015

Standing beside the main road is the priory church of All Saints, the only substantial remaining part of the priory, whose ruins extend east of the church. The Wayside Café (left), a typical refreshment halt of its time, has been redeveloped into houses, and the single petrol pump on the roadside beyond it would now not be allowed.

◄ **WEYBOURNE**
The Street c1960
W353030

The old farmhouse belonging to the Jennings and Monument families became a hotel in 1947 and has remained a popular venue for tourists. Fifty years on, the road and street look the same, and probably, apart from the cars and telegraph pole, looked the same a hundred and fifty years ago.

► **CLEY-NEXT-THE-SEA**
The Windmill c1955
C118011

Overlooking the salt marshes of Cley Bird Sanctuary, the 18th-century windmill last ground corn about 1920. Subsequently most working parts were removed, and it became a guest house. The sails, fanstage and galleries have since been replaced, and the mill and its surrounding buildings have become unusual venues for holiday accommodation.

CLEY-NEXT-THE-SEA
High Street c1955
C118013

A narrow, twisting road winds through the picturesque village of Cley, with its flint, brick and colourwashed houses. The George Hotel (centre) stands where the road turns sharply towards the windmill. Formerly a flourishing port at the mouth of the Glaven, exporting wool and grain to London and the continent, Cley can now be reached only by very small craft.

SALTHOUSE
Post Office Corner c1955 S507006

A superb view across the salt marshes towards the sea was unobstructed by the mound of shingle which now forms a sea wall, built after the sea flooded the village in 1953. The post office remains in the far cottage, but the petrol pump (right) would be illegal nowadays. The dark marks on the marsh are probably hides for birdwatchers.

SALTHOUSE
The View from the Marshes c1955
S507009

The stretch of water running alongside the road is draining the marshes to enable them to be grazed. Ducks, swans, geese and many less common birds make this a popular area with ornithologists. The chapel on the right of the picture is now a private house.

▲ **SALTHOUSE,** *The Manor House and the Church c1955* S507005

On a slight hill above the village stands the 15th-century church of St Nicholas, with its glorious clear light-bringing windows, and its tower built in the 13th century. When the sea inundated the village in 1953, the small population fled up to the church for safety.

◄ **GLANDFORD**
The Church c1960
G209080

Perched on a gentle hill beside the Glaven, and seen here across a field of sugar beet, St Martin's church was virtually a ruin until it was rebuilt about 1900 by Sir Alfred Jodrell. Inside, there are stained glass windows by Kempe and exceptionally fine and prolific carvings, including a full rood screen and roof angels, in local oak and cedar. The churchyard is a wildlife conservation area.

▼ **WIVETON,** *The Church and the Bridge c1955* W356004

The river Glaven ambles its way through meadowland and under the single-track, humped bridge on the road to Cley. Wiveton church, with its onion finials on the square tower and prominent row of clerestory windows, looks across to Cley church and Blakeney church, each only a short walk across the marshland.

► **LANGHAM**
Post Office Corner c1955 L314001

Langham is a tiny village, scarcely more than a crossroads. The lantern over the gateway to the church of St Andrew and St Mary has gone, but it is perhaps surprising that the post office beyond the signpost is still functioning - so is the village hall opposite.

◄ **BLAKENEY**
The Ship Inn 1925
77527

Blakeney is a picturesque coastal village at the estuary of the river Glaven. This is a popular sailing and walking area, especially out to Blakeney Point, a spit of land round which many seals cavort. The narrow High Street winds down to Blakeney quay. The Ship Inn, halfway down the street on the left, has been transformed into Ship Cottage and Benbow Cottage, but The White Horse beyond is still popular with visitors. The history of the lovely flint and brick house (right) is preserved in its present name, Bank Cottage. Notice the narrow tyres and folded-down hood of the car.

► **BLAKENEY**
The Village 1933 85837

This part of the coast is said to have been a haunt of smugglers who were guided to safety by a light in a second small tower of Blakeney church. Here we have a view of the creek down which swiftly flowing tides carry sailing boats out to Blakeney Harbour, an expanse of open sea sheltered by a narrow sandbar, culminating in Blakeney Point. The Guildhall Café, named after a medieval merchant's house, of which the brick and flint cellar can still be seen, has been redeveloped into flats.

BLAKENEY
The Quay 1925
77526

The creek at low tide afforded a muddy playground for children. At high tide they enjoy dipping for crabs from the roadside in front of The Blakeney Hotel. Notice the men wearing jackets, ties and hats.

BLAKENEY
The Village c1955
B121052

It is twenty years after photograph No 85837 (page 73), and the Guildhall Café has a smart new sign and bay windows. It is almost low tide in the creek, and across the harbour we can just see the old lifeboat house on the horizon. A travelling fair has arrived with an amusements tent and a merry-go-round giving rides in cars or on horses.

STIFFKEY, *The Townshend Arms c1955* S193013

Named after the river Stiff, this small village is famous for 'Stookey Blues' – Norfolk cockles. The Townshend Arms was 'highly commended for unusually good cooking' under Mr and Mrs Cooper in the 1920s and 30s, but it has been a private house since 1960. The cart shed (which displays the bus timetable, right) is now a fascinating shop selling antique lamps.

HOLKHAM
The Victoria Hotel c1965 H340001

Belonging to the Holkham estate, the home of the Earl and Countess of Leicester, this square, flint-built hotel stands at the entrance to the drive of the magnificent Palladian mansion. Facing north towards the sea, it surveys the area of coastal conservation instigated by the Earl's ancestor, the great agriculturalist, Coke of Norfolk.

BURNHAM MARKET, *The Village c1955* B500008

Viewed from the east, St Mary's church with its battlemented, 13th-century tower, looks down the main street towards the war memorial. A stream bubbles alongside the main road, and the well-mown grassy areas give a spacious feel to the village.

BURNHAM MARKET
The Village c1955
B500003

The north side of the High Street shows The Hoste Arms, a 17th-century coaching inn which has been variously a court house, a livestock market and a brothel. Horatio Nelson, whose birthplace was at nearby Burnham Thorpe, regularly picked up his mail at The Hoste. Today the street would be crowded with cars, and certainly more than the single Hubbards coach.

◄ **BURNHAM OVERY**
The Village c1960
B819018

Here we see an interesting meeting place of roads in the middle of the small village. St Clements church with its unusual belfry atop its square tower lies beyond the bend in the Wells road. The Brother's Cross on the road island has suffered from centuries of weathering, while the cottage on the left is unusually decorated with stone busts – is it the house of a retired sea captain?

◀ **BURNHAM MARKET**
The Village c1955 B500004

We are looking at the opposite side of the road from picture No B500003 (page 79); a row of mainly Georgian houses gives a gracious air to the village. The steep angle of some of the roofs indicate that they were probably previously thatched, implying that the building is earlier than it outwardly appears.

▲ **BURNHAM OVERY STAITHE,** *Post Office Corner c1955* O80002

Jimmy Richards' shop and post office (left) could supply most of the needs of the villagers – Winalot dog food, Wills Capstan cigarettes, Brooke Bond tea, Lyons tea – which now have to be bought in Burnham Market. All the buildings in this photograph have been demolished, and the only shop in the village is the chandlery on the quayside.

◀ **BURNHAM OVERY STAITHE**
The Village c1955
O80001

All that remains of this row of brick built cottages is the section on the right, known as Rose Cottage. The larger part has been replaced by a modern house, which retains the old name of The Hollies. It is remarkable that the chimney stacks have no pots surmounting them.

WEST NORFOLK

NORTH and south of King's Lynn, west Norfolk is wide, open countryside bordering on the flat fenlands of Lincolnshire and Cambridge. The Wash laps the west coast, which is a popular area with tourists, but to the south there are few trees to intercept the winds blowing coldly from the north and east. The fields of rich, black earth are cut by dykes draining the water into rivers and cuts.

OLD HUNSTANTON, *The Old Bridge c1955* O119100

This delightful rustic scene on the edge of the village shows flat agricultural land, liberally planted with trees. In spite of the demands of modern traffic, the old stone bridge has survived. A girl is resting on the buttress, enjoying the peaceful scene: cows in the field and Queen Anne's Lace and marguerites decorating the verges.

OLD HUNSTANTON *The Neptune Hotel c1960* O119102

Cars with shiny back bumpers date the picture of this old village inn, now smartened with a new sign and a wall to replace the palings, while 'Real Ales and Fine Wines' replace sponsorship by Morgan's brewery.

HEACHAM, *High Street c1955* H57042

Heacham, now probably more famous for its lavender fields, was the home village of John Rolfe, whose life was saved by the Red Indian Princess Pocahontas. They married in 1614 and came back to Heacham Hall. Sad to say, she died a year later on a return journey to visit her people in America. Most of the these solid brick buildings are still identifiable: the white-painted public house, advertising Bullards Ales and Stout, is a private house, but the old bowling green and toilet building can be glimpsed behind. The extinct National Provincial Bank (left) has become a house agent; next door, here advertising Gold Flake tobacco, is the Card Cabin.

▼ **HEACHAM,** *The High House c1955* H57060

We are looking at the rear view of this old house on the right of the picture. Three storeys, visible at the front, no doubt give the name to the house. The more modern building on the left has been demolished to make way for blocks of flats.

► **SNETTISHAM**
The Church 1896 38648

With its solid, square tower surmounted by a tremendous, soaring spire, St Mary's church is visible for miles around Snettisham. Three pointed arches and a magnificent window on the west front prepare the visitor for the immense, cathedral-like interior. The pulpit has unusual painted panels, and the pillars are surrounded by stone seats.

◄ **SNETTISHAM**
Market Place c1955 S464017

The magnificent chestnut tree beside the bus shelter has been replaced (but not forgotten) by a sign showing the Snettisham torc and with the inscription 'Site of the Old Chestnut Tree 22 June 1992'. The Stores is prominently advertising Woodbines and Players cigarettes. Behind the war memorial on the right is now the Old Bank Coffee Shop.

► **INGOLDISTHORPE**
The Church c1955
I45007

Only fifty years ago the church of St Michael and All Angels stood guardian over a rural village, next to a farm with solid buildings, a field of sheep and abundant wild flowers. Now it is tucked away, barely visible behind trees in the midst of a warren of new houses.

DERSINGHAM, *The Village Sign c1965* D148018

Bright yellow lions rampant support the coat of arms, while a bright blue background and fishes emphasise the close connection with the sea. Embedded in a brick and flint plinth, the town sign was presented by Dersingham Women's Institute in 1967.

DERSINGHAM
Manor Road c1965
D148021

The main road into the village of Dersingham is unrecognisable from this photograph. The semi-detached Edwardian houses are now surrounded by streets of new dwellings. The old-style name sign beside the narrow highway reflects a time before the influx of holidaymakers to the area.

DERSINGHAM, *The Memorial and Station Road c1965* D148010

Two lions stand guard at the stone memorial to those who died in two world wars. The large playing field now includes a children's play park. Traffic lights now regulate the crossroads, and the 'No Through Road' sign has been replaced by an internationally recognised symbolic one.

► **SANDRINGHAM**
The Church 1896
38402

The tiny church of St Mary Magdalene in the grounds of Sandringham House was rebuilt in the 16th century and renovated by King Edward VII. The superb solid silver altar and reredos were presented to Queen Alexandra in his memory. The Royal Family regularly worship here when they are in residence, but like many rural churches it now shares a vicar with neighbouring churches.

◄ **WOLFERTON**
The Village 1921
71062

Light browny-red carr stone and flint are the only natural building materials found locally, though bricks have been made from local clay since Roman times. The carr-stone wall on the right is a fine example of a builder's work. The pretty thatched bus shelter in front of the Wolferton Social Club has disappeared, sad to say.

▲ **WOLFERTON,** *The Station c1955* W354001

When trains still ran north from King's Lynn, Wolferton station was where royal parties alighted for Sandringham. The signal box is on the left of the picture, and the main station buildings, including Queen Victoria's waiting room, are on the right. They are now a private residence, but the clock still ticks.

◄ **WOLFERTON**
The Post Office c1955
W354022

White posts still show where these gates guarded the drive to the post office. The buildings, with their timber decoration characteristic of the Sandringham estate village, are now private houses. The station clock can be seen on the right, above the wavy edge of the platform canopy.

CLENCHWARTON
The Village c1965
C416011

This long, straggling village just to the west of King's Lynn is a delightful backwater on the estuary of the River Ouse. The Wheelwrights Arms is basically an old house modernised in pre-war days. It is now a private house conveniently close to the row of small shops and the church. The sign warning of schoolchildren crossing has been updated.

CLENCHWARTON, *The Post Office c1965* C416014

Safety requirements would preclude the sale of paraffin on the casual self-service basis we see here (right), nor are cigarettes now freely available from the Embassy dispenser outside the Post Office. Pre-decimalisation prices appear ridiculously low today – ceiling paper is 3s 11d a roll (about 20p), and a decorator's table is 45s 6d (about £2.25).

CASTLE ACRE, *Bailey Street c1955* C41005

This 13th-century gateway was built to defend the north entrance to a planned town adjoining the west side of the castle. Substantial round flint towers buttress the arches on each side. The road winds down through the village towards the remains of the castle.

TEN MILE BANK
The Village c1955
T225005

Leading from the main village towards the church, this row of cottages reflects the stark nature of the countryside. Cement washed walls and slate roofs are not usual in other parts of Norfolk.

◀ **TEN MILE BANK**
The Church c1955 T225007

The bank on the right of the picture leads up to the River Great Ouse. The clear glass windows of St Mark's church look far over the flat fenlands to spectacular sunsets. What is unusual here is that the bell is pulled on the outside of the church.

▲ **HILGAY,** *The Church c1960* H308019

Two identical lych gates, separated by a long avenue of holly and lime trees, lead up to All Saints' church. Like many Norfolk churches, it has a square, battlemented tower and is lovingly cared for by a small congregation. There is an interesting marble pulpit, and an old bier, with its glass cover intact, stands at the back of the church.

◀ **STOWBRIDGE**
The Village c1965
S689001

This is another unrepeatable photograph. The road was moved and a new, wide bridge over the Great Ouse was opened in July 2002. Bethesda Chapel, built in 1860, is now a private house, but at least the fenland view remains.

NARBOROUGH
The Bridge and the River c1955 N189015

This delightful village has been greatly redeveloped in recent years. The cottages adjoining the butcher's shop by the River Nar and the small post office where villagers would gather for a chat have been replaced by modern bungalows.

NARBOROUGH, *The Ship Inn c1955* N189026

Standing squarely beside the road to Pentney, the pub (centre) is a relic of old Narborough. Vin and Everett's maltings (left), where barley was processed before being transported by barge along the Nar, has been replaced by a doctor's surgery. The fence on the left enclosed cottages and their garden: the plot is now a petrol station.

BRECKLAND

THE south-west of Norfolk has a distinct character. There are large forested areas on the sandy, chalk soil. There is much evidence of prehistoric man, and signs of his flint knapping can be seen at Grimes Graves.

HINGHAM, *The Market Place c1955* H309013

In the centre of Hingham lovely Georgian houses surround the green, which glows with daffodils at springtime. The village sign, commemorating the Coronation of Queen Elizabeth II, represents 200 emigrants from Hingham to the New World between 1633 and 1643, among them ancestors of Abraham Lincoln. A mounting block in the Market Place is a gift from Hingham, Massachusetts, replacing one given to them in reverse in 1911.

WATTON
High Street c1950
W383002

A market town rather than a village, Watton has a constant stream of traffic through its bustling centre. The attempt to impose parking on one side of the street on alternate days has long since been abandoned in favour of time limits. There is a good variety of shops shielding their goods from sun damage with old fashioned canvas blinds.

WATTON, *The Clock Tower c1950* W383003

In the centre of the High Street stands the unusual clock tower surmounted by a weather vane; it depicts a hare, for which the local name is a 'watt', and a barrel, a 'tun', giving 'Watton'. Just south of the town is Wayland Wood, reputed to be the site of the Babes in the Wood, who are depicted in the town sign.

GREAT ELLINGHAM *Post Office Corner c1955* G191005

A fine, traditionally thatched house stood in the centre of the village opposite the post office, which can be identified on the right by its telephone box. The chestnut tree on the left still produces conkers, but the land and barn behind now house three new bungalows.

METHWOLD, *High Street c1965* M229008

St George's church, in the centre of the village, dominates from every quarter. It is a fine building with 16th-century clerestory windows. On the square tower the clock bears in gold letters the admonition: 'Man know thyself.' The building facing up the wide High Street is the George.

METHWOLD
The Village c1965
M229011

The spire on the church tower dominates from this direction also. Small shops can be discerned, one on each side of the road. The house on the right has a protruding upper storey, which may indicate a that it is a timber-framed building – or it could be that passing traffic has damaged the lower part.

▼ **MUNDFORD,** *The Church from Thetford Road c1955* M310002

This view looks across open playing fields, which still provide a valuable amenity for this charming village. The war memorial (centre) is surmounted by a crucifix, and commemorates those from the nearby Lynford Estate who fell in the two World Wars. The road junction has now been realigned, and there is a great deal of new housing in the village.

► **LYNFORD** *The Roman Catholic Church c1955* L523019

Hidden in the forest on the Lynford estate, the little church of Our Lady of Consolation and St Stephen sits solidly among the trees. Built mainly of local flint, the buttresses and corners are strengthened with stone. Stone is also used for the small round spire and the decorative roof gully.

MUNDFORD
The Street c1960 M310010

The old village centre is exactly the same now as it was in 1960. Probably little has changed since the cottages were built in 1885. Note the charming bay windows, the gabled roof with pretty tiling and the interesting chimneys on the first flint cottage; there is a thatched roof on the next, followed by another row of bay windowed, gabled cottages, altogether making a delightful street.

◀ **GREAT HOCKHAM**
The Village c1955
G192001

Wishing Well Cottage on the left of the picture shows a Norfolk thatcher's work at its best, sitting like a comfortable hat on the old walls. On the right, behind the signpost, is the old school, which was built in Victorian times. The village has a lovely green at its centre.

◀ ICKBURGH
The Church c1960 I77007

The tiny village of Ickburgh supports with great care the lovely church of St Peter. Inside are angels in the roof, small pews for children and an unusual stone screen and pulpit. The parapet of the tower is decorated with chequered stonework.

▲ EAST HARLING, *The Village c1965* E132007

This rather nondescript street of terraced cottages is known as Gallants Lane. The buildings on the right are probably the oldest, and the chapel beside the car (right) is dated 1889. The white-painted row is probably the newest; even so, these cottages have now been updated for the 21st century with new windows and doors.

◀ GARBOLDISHAM
The Village c1955
G188002

The road bends round the church of St John the Baptist towards the school. Perhaps the lady on the left is walking up to collect her child. The cottage on the right is the Old Shoemakers House, and beyond that is a superb new village hall.

SOUTH NORFOLK

THE area south of Norwich towards the Waveney valley is gently rolling, softly wooded countryside, enfolding many pretty villages.

BRAMERTON, *The Church c1955* B301002

Pass through the thatched lych gate into the quiet churchyard and enter a tiny 13th-century village church. Westminster chimes strike each quarter hour from the clock in the bell tower. A north transept and several stained glass windows were added in Victorian times, and we can admire a beautiful 14th-century font bowl. Sad to say, the church brasses were stolen in 1993, but trustingly the church remains unlocked.

BRAMERTON
The Woods End c1955 B301007

A long, winding lane leads down to this quiet stretch of the River Yare, east of Norwich, and the Woods End public house. Built in 1895, it was owned by Morgan's Brewery, then by Bass. It now has a gravelled picnic area bordering the river, enlivened by numerous ducks and gulls, and is a popular place to relax for visitors arriving by boat or by car.

FRAMINGHAM EARL, *The Post Office c1960* F129005

The mainly residential village of Framingham Earl stretches along the main road from Norwich to Bungay. Houses have long since been built over Oaklands Farm, whose produce supplied the local stores. In the 1960s Green Shield stamps offered an incentive to buy vegetables, bread, paraffin, calor gas, stamps, and Birds Eye frozen foods. Today, a 'One Stop Convenience Store' offers an even more eclectic array of goods.

GILLINGHAM, *The Old Church 1894* 33346

Over a hundred years after this photograph was taken, the old ivy-covered tower still stands like a sleeping beauty amid weather-washed gravestones. In these remains of an early church, there are signs of an overlap between Saxon and Norman styles. Why did it become a ruin? Were the stones used to build the newer, possibly 17th-century church beside it? Or was Gillingham originally a double parish?

STARSTON
The View from the Church c1955 S468007

The main road now bypasses this delightful village, where the river runs alongside the street. The bridge, with its neat brickwork and wooden parapets, appears to have been recently built. The building glimpsed through trees on the left is Starston Jubilee Hall, and a village sign was placed beside it in 1980. The large, colourwashed house is more characteristic of nearby Suffolk than Norfolk.

STARSTON, *The Village c1955* S468004

Trees line the main street at the bottom of the hill leading to the church. The furthest visible house has an interesting stepped gable, and the variety of individual cottages gives character to the village. Outside the post office a delivery man is unloading sacks of coal.

open

SCOLE
Main Street c1965
S508012

Just over the border from Suffolk, traffic used to be squeezed through this crossroads village. A bypass now frees The Scole Inn, built as The White Hart Inn in 1655, from noise and fume pollution. In its heyday this fine, Dutch gabled building (in the centre of the photograph) boasted a great round bed to accommodate 30 travellers from the 40 coaches which paused here each day.

SCOLE, *The Old Bridge c1965* S508011

This beautiful old bridge spanning the River Waveney was destroyed in 1990. It was no longer safe, and repairs were said to be too costly. With its wicket-fence parapet and tie bar plates as decorative as they are practical, it was an attractive feature enjoyed by fishermen, walkers and nature lovers.

SCOLE
Old Beams c1965
S508015

A row of old thatched cottages stands beside the former main road from Ipswich to Norwich, facing the road west to Diss. A younger building on the left makes a contrast with its tiled roof, brick structure and conspicuous downpipe. The line of decorative brickwork between the floors adds interest. The petrol station has now been redeveloped into a housing complex.

LONG STRATTON, *The Village c1960* L300006

Entering the village from the south, traffic was reduced to 40mph (left) – the limit is now 30mph. The Belvedere stores on the right was housed in a row of three cottages, probably dating back to the 15th century. The steep angle of the roof indicates that it was originally thatched, but the chimneys have obviously been renewed. An antique shop now attracts visitors here.

LONG STRATTON
The Village c1955 L300012

At the far end of the village, we are still looking ahead up the hill towards Norwich. Cars and even Tye Trailers from York (extreme right) found room to park. A constant stream of traffic now thunders right through the village. Buildings, including the Swan Hotel, remain much as they were in 1955; but the new house we can see in the trees was the beginning of new residential estates.

INDEX

Frith Book Co Titles

www.francisfrith.co.uk

The Frith Book Company publishes over 100 new titles each year. A selection of those currently available is listed below. For latest catalogue please contact Frith Book Co.
Town Books 96 pages, approximately 100 photos. ***County and Themed Books*** 128 pages, approximately 150 photos (unless specified). All titles hardback with laminated case and jacket, except those indicated pb (paperback)

Amersham, Chesham & Rickmansworth (pb)	1-85937-340-2	£9.99
Andover (pb)	1-85937-292-9	£9.99
Aylesbury (pb)	1-85937-227-9	£9.99
Barnstaple (pb)	1-85937-300-3	£9.99
Basildon Living Memories (pb)	1-85937-515-4	£9.99
Bath (pb)	1-85937-419-0	£9.99
Bedford (pb)	1-85937-205-8	£9.99
Bedfordshire Living Memories	1-85937-513-8	£14.99
Belfast (pb)	1-85937-303-8	£9.99
Berkshire (pb)	1-85937-191-4	£9.99
Berkshire Churches	1-85937-170-1	£17.99
Berkshire Living Memories	1-85937-332-1	£14.99
Black Country	1-85937-497-2	£12.99
Blackpool (pb)	1-85937-393-3	£9.99
Bognor Regis (pb)	1-85937-431-x	£9.99
Bournemouth (pb)	1-85937-545-6	£9.99
Bradford (pb)	1-85937-204-x	£9.99
Bridgend (pb)	1-85937-386-0	£7.99
Bridgwater (pb)	1-85937-305-4	£9.99
Bridport (pb)	1-85937-327-5	£9.99
Brighton (pb)	1-85937-192-2	£8.99
Bristol (pb)	1-85937-264-3	£9.99
British Life A Century Ago (pb)	1-85937-213-9	£9.99
Buckinghamshire (pb)	1-85937-200-7	£9.99
Camberley (pb)	1-85937-222-8	£9.99
Cambridge (pb)	1-85937-422-0	£9.99
Cambridgeshire (pb)	1-85937-420-4	£9.99
Cambridgeshire Villages	1-85937-523-5	£14.99
Canals And Waterways (pb)	1-85937-291-0	£9.99
Canterbury Cathedral (pb)	1-85937-179-5	£9.99
Cardiff (pb)	1-85937-093-4	£9.99
Carmarthenshire (pb)	1-85937-604-5	£9.99
Chelmsford (pb)	1-85937-310-0	£9.99
Cheltenham (pb)	1-85937-095-0	£9.99
Cheshire (pb)	1-85937-271-6	£9.99
Chester (pb)	1-85937-382 8	£9.99
Chesterfield (pb)	1-85937-378-x	£9.99
Chichester (pb)	1-85937-228-7	£9.99
Churches of East Cornwall (pb)	1-85937-249-x	£9.99
Churches of Hampshire (pb)	1-85937-207-4	£9.99
Cinque Ports & Two Ancient Towns	1-85937-492-1	£14.99
Colchester (pb)	1-85937-188-4	£8.99
Cornwall (pb)	1-85937-229-5	£9.99
Cornwall Living Memories	1-85937-248-1	£14.99
Cotswolds (pb)	1-85937-230-9	£9.99
Cotswolds Living Memories	1-85937-255-4	£14.99
County Durham (pb)	1-85937-398-4	£9.99
Croydon Living Memories (pb)	1-85937-162-0	£9.99
Cumbria (pb)	1-85937-621-5	£9.99
Derby (pb)	1-85937-367-4	£9.99
Derbyshire (pb)	1-85937-196-5	£9.99
Derbyshire Living Memories	1-85937-330-5	£14.99
Devon (pb)	1-85937-297-x	£9.99
Devon Churches (pb)	1-85937-250-3	£9.99
Dorchester (pb)	1-85937-307-0	£9.99
Dorset (pb)	1-85937-269-4	£9.99
Dorset Coast (pb)	1-85937-299-6	£9.99
Dorset Living Memories (pb)	1-85937-584-7	£9.99
Down the Severn (pb)	1-85937-560-x	£9.99
Down The Thames (pb)	1-85937-278-3	£9.99
Down the Trent	1-85937-311-9	£14.99
East Anglia (pb)	1-85937-265-1	£9.99
East Grinstead (pb)	1-85937-138-8	£9.99
East London	1-85937-080-2	£14.99
East Sussex (pb)	1-85937-606-1	£9.99
Eastbourne (pb)	1-85937-399-2	£9.99
Edinburgh (pb)	1-85937-193-0	£8.99
England In The 1880s	1-85937-331-3	£17.99
Essex - Second Selection	1-85937-456-5	£14.99
Essex (pb)	1-85937-270-8	£9.99
Essex Coast	1-85937-342-9	£14.99
Essex Living Memories	1-85937-490-5	£14.99
Exeter	1-85937-539-1	£9.99
Exmoor (pb)	1-85937-608-8	£9.99
Falmouth (pb)	1-85937-594-4	£9.99
Folkestone (pb)	1-85937-124-8	£9.99
Frome (pb)	1-85937-317-8	£9.99
Glamorgan	1-85937-488-3	£14.99
Glasgow (pb)	1-85937-190-6	£9.99
Glastonbury (pb)	1-85937-338-0	£7.99
Gloucester (pb)	1-85937-232-5	£9.99
Gloucestershire (pb)	1-85937-561-8	£9.99
Great Yarmouth (pb)	1-85937-426-3	£9.99
Greater Manchester (pb)	1-85937-266-x	£9.99
Guildford (pb)	1-85937-410-7	£9.99
Hampshire (pb)	1-85937-279-1	£9.99
Harrogate (pb)	1-85937-423-9	£9.99
Hastings and Bexhill (pb)	1-85937-131-0	£9.99
Heart of Lancashire (pb)	1-85937-197-3	£9.99
Helston (pb)	1-85937-214-7	£9.99
Hereford (pb)	1-85937-175-2	£9.99
Herefordshire (pb)	1-85937-567-7	£9.99
Herefordshire Living Memories	1-85937-514-6	£14.99
Hertfordshire (pb)	1-85937-247-3	£9.99
Horsham (pb)	1-85937-432-8	£9.99
Humberside (pb)	1-85937-605-3	£9.99
Hythe, Romney Marsh, Ashford (pb)	1-85937-256-2	£9.99
Ipswich (pb)	1-85937-424-7	£9.99
Isle of Man (pb)	1-85937-268-6	£9.99
Isle of Wight (pb)	1-85937-429-8	£9.99
Isle of Wight Living Memories	1-85937-304-6	£14.99
Kent (pb)	1-85937-189-2	£9.99
Kent Living Memories(pb)	1-85937-401-8	£9.99
Kings Lynn (pb)	1-85937-334-8	£9.99

Available from your local bookshop or from the publisher

Frith Book Co Titles (continued)

Lake District (pb)	1-85937-275-9	£9.99
Lancashire Living Memories	1-85937-335-6	£14.99
Lancaster, Morecambe, Heysham (pb)	1-85937-233-3	£9.99
Leeds (pb)	1-85937-202-3	£9.99
Leicester (pb)	1-85937-381-x	£9.99
Leicestershire & Rutland Living Memories	1-85937-500-6	£12.99
Leicestershire (pb)	1-85937-185-x	£9.99
Lighthouses	1-85937-257-0	£9.99
Lincoln (pb)	1-85937-380-1	£9.99
Lincolnshire (pb)	1-85937-433-6	£9.99
Liverpool and Merseyside (pb)	1-85937-234-1	£9.99
London (pb)	1-85937-183-3	£9.99
London Living Memories	1-85937-454-9	£14.99
Ludlow (pb)	1-85937-176-0	£9.99
Luton (pb)	1-85937-235-x	£9.99
Maidenhead (pb)	1-85937-339-9	£9.99
Maidstone (pb)	1-85937-391-7	£9.99
Manchester (pb)	1-85937-198-1	£9.99
Marlborough (pb)	1-85937-336-4	£9.99
Middlesex	1-85937-158-2	£14.99
Monmouthshire	1-85937-532-4	£14.99
New Forest (pb)	1-85937-390-9	£9.99
Newark (pb)	1-85937-366-6	£9.99
Newport, Wales (pb)	1-85937-258-9	£9.99
Newquay (pb)	1-85937-421-2	£9.99
Norfolk (pb)	1-85937-195-7	£9.99
Norfolk Broads	1-85937-486-7	£14.99
Norfolk Living Memories (pb)	1-85937-402-6	£9.99
North Buckinghamshire	1-85937-626-6	£14.99
North Devon Living Memories	1-85937-261-9	£14.99
North Hertfordshire	1-85937-547-2	£14.99
North London (pb)	1-85937-403-4	£9.99
North Somerset	1-85937-302-x	£14.99
North Wales (pb)	1-85937-298-8	£9.99
North Yorkshire (pb)	1-85937-236-8	£9.99
Northamptonshire Living Memories	1-85937-529-4	£14.99
Northamptonshire	1-85937-150-7	£14.99
Northumberland Tyne & Wear (pb)	1-85937-281-3	£9.99
Northumberland	1-85937-522-7	£14.99
Norwich (pb)	1-85937-194-9	£8.99
Nottingham (pb)	1-85937-324-0	£9.99
Nottinghamshire (pb)	1-85937-187-6	£9.99
Oxford (pb)	1-85937-411-5	£9.99
Oxfordshire (pb)	1-85937-430-1	£9.99
Oxfordshire Living Memories	1-85937-525-1	£14.99
Paignton (pb)	1-85937-374-7	£7.99
Peak District (pb)	1-85937-280-5	£9.99
Pembrokeshire	1-85937-262-7	£14.99
Penzance (pb)	1-85937-595-2	£9.99
Peterborough (pb)	1-85937-219-8	£9.99
Picturesque Harbours	1-85937-208-2	£14.99
Piers	1-85937-237-6	£17.99
Plymouth (pb)	1-85937-389-5	£9.99
Poole & Sandbanks (pb)	1-85937-251-1	£9.99
Preston (pb)	1-85937-212-0	£9.99
Reading (pb)	1-85937-238-4	£9.99
Redhill to Reigate (pb)	1-85937-596-0	£9.99
Ringwood (pb)	1-85937-384-4	£7.99
Romford (pb)	1-85937-319-4	£9.99
Royal Tunbridge Wells (pb)	1-85937-504-9	£9.99
Salisbury (pb)	1-85937-239-2	£9.99
Scarborough (pb)	1-85937-379-8	£9.99
Sevenoaks and Tonbridge (pb)	1-85937-392-5	£9.99
Sheffield & South Yorks (pb)	1-85937-267-8	£9.99
Sherborne (pb)	1-85937-301-1	£9.99
Shrewsbury (pb)	1-85937-325-9	£9.99
Shropshire (pb)	1-85937-326-7	£9.99
Shropshire Living Memories	1-85937-643-6	£14.99
Somerset	1-85937-153-1	£14.99
South Devon Coast	1-85937-107-8	£14.99
South Devon Living Memories (pb)	1-85937-609-6	£9.99
South East London (pb)	1-85937-263-5	£9.99
South Somerset	1-85937-318-6	£14.99
South Wales	1-85937-519-7	£14.99
Southampton (pb)	1-85937-427-1	£9.99
Southend (pb)	1-85937-313-5	£9.99
Southport (pb)	1-85937-425-5	£9.99
St Albans (pb)	1-85937-341-0	£9.99
St Ives (pb)	1-85937-415-8	£9.99
Stafford Living Memories (pb)	1-85937-503-0	£9.99
Staffordshire (pb)	1-85937-308-9	£9.99
Stourbridge (pb)	1-85937-530-8	£9.99
Stratford upon Avon (pb)	1-85937-388-7	£9.99
Suffolk (pb)	1-85937-221-x	£9.99
Suffolk Coast (pb)	1-85937-610-x	£9.99
Surrey (pb)	1-85937-240-6	£9.99
Surrey Living Memories	1-85937-328-3	£14.99
Sussex (pb)	1-85937-184-1	£9.99
Sutton (pb)	1-85937-337-2	£9.99
Swansea (pb)	1-85937-167-1	£9.99
Taunton (pb)	1-85937-314-3	£9.99
Tees Valley & Cleveland (pb)	1-85937-623-1	£9.99
Teignmouth (pb)	1-85937-370-4	£7.99
Thanet (pb)	1-85937-116-7	£9.99
Tiverton (pb)	1-85937-178-7	£9.99
Torbay (pb)	1-85937-597-9	£9.99
Truro (pb)	1-85937-598-7	£9.99
Victorian & Edwardian Dorset	1-85937-254-6	£14.99
Victorian & Edwardian Kent (pb)	1-85937-624-X	£9.99
Victorian & Edwardian Maritime Album (pb)	1-85937-622-3	£9.99
Victorian and Edwardian Sussex (pb)	1-85937-625-8	£9.99
Villages of Devon (pb)	1-85937-293-7	£9.99
Villages of Kent (pb)	1-85937-294-5	£9.99
Villages of Sussex (pb)	1-85937-295-3	£9.99
Warrington (pb)	1-85937-507-3	£9.99
Warwick (pb)	1-85937-518-9	£9.99
Warwickshire (pb)	1-85937-203-1	£9.99
Welsh Castles (pb)	1-85937-322-4	£9.99
West Midlands (pb)	1-85937-289-9	£9.99
West Sussex (pb)	1-85937-607-x	£9.99
West Yorkshire (pb)	1-85937-201-5	£9.99
Weston Super Mare (pb)	1-85937-306-2	£9.99
Weymouth (pb)	1-85937-209-0	£9.99
Wiltshire (pb)	1-85937-277-5	£9.99
Wiltshire Churches (pb)	1-85937-171-x	£9.99
Wiltshire Living Memories (pb)	1-85937-396-8	£9.99
Winchester (pb)	1-85937-428-x	£9.99
Windsor (pb)	1-85937-333-x	£9.99
Wokingham & Bracknell (pb)	1-85937-329-1	£9.99
Woodbridge (pb)	1-85937-498-0	£9.99
Worcester (pb)	1-85937-165-5	£9.99
Worcestershire Living Memories	1-85937-489-1	£14.99
Worcestershire	1-85937-152-3	£14.99
York (pb)	1-85937-199-x	£9.99
Yorkshire (pb)	1-85937-186-8	£9.99
Yorkshire Coastal Memories	1-85937-506-5	£14.99
Yorkshire Dales	1-85937-502-2	£14.99
Yorkshire Living Memories (pb)	1-85937-397-6	£9.99

See Frith books on the internet at www.francisfrith.co.uk

Frith Products & Services

Francis Frith would doubtless be pleased to know that the pioneering publishing venture he started in 1860 still continues today. Over a hundred and forty years later, The Francis Frith Collection continues in the same innovative tradition and is now one of the foremost publishers of vintage photographs in the world. Some of the current activities include:

Interior Decoration

Today Frith's photographs can be seen framed and as giant wall murals in thousands of pubs, restaurants, hotels, banks, retail stores and other public buildings throughout the country. In every case they enhance the unique local atmosphere of the places they depict and provide reminders of gentler days in an increasingly busy and frenetic world.

Product Promotions

Frith products are used by many major companies to promote the sales of their own products or to reinforce their own history and heritage. Frith promotions have been used by Hovis bread, Courage beers, Scots Porage Oats, Colman's mustard, Cadbury's foods, Mellow Birds coffee, Dunhill pipe tobacco, Guinness, and Bulmer's Cider.

Genealogy and Family History

As the interest in family history and roots grows world-wide, more and more people are turning to Frith's photographs of Great Britain for images of the towns, villages and streets where their ancestors lived; and, of course, photographs of the churches and chapels where their ancestors were christened, married and buried are an essential part of every genealogy tree and family album.

Frith Products

All Frith photographs are available Framed or just as Mounted Prints and Posters (size 23 x 16 inches). These may be ordered from the address below. From time to time other products - Address Books, Calendars, Table Mats, etc - are available.

The Internet

Already fifty thousand Frith photographs can be viewed and purchased on the internet through the Frith websites and a myriad of partner sites.

For more detailed information on Frith companies and products, look at these sites:

www.francisfrith.co.uk
www.francisfrith.com
(for North American visitors)

See the complete list of Frith Books at:

www.francisfrith.co.uk

This web site is regularly updated with the latest list of publications from the Frith Book Company. If you wish to buy books relating to another part of the country that your local bookshop does not stock, you may purchase on-line.

For further information, trade, or author enquiries please contact us at the address below:

The Francis Frith Collection, Frith's Barn, Teffont, Salisbury, Wiltshire, England SP3 5QP.
Tel: +44 (0)1722 716 376 Fax: +44 (0)1722 716 881 Email: sales@francisfrith.co.uk

See Frith books on the internet at www.francisfrith.co.uk

FREE MOUNTED PRINT

Mounted Print
Overall size 14 x 11 inches

Fill in and cut out this voucher and return *it with your remittance for £2.25 (to cover postage and handling). Offer valid for delivery to UK addresses only.*

Choose any photograph included in this book. *Your SEPIA print will be A4 in size. It will be mounted in a cream mount with a burgundy rule line (overall size 14 x 11 inches).*

Order additional Mounted Prints at HALF PRICE (only £7.49 each*)
If you would like to order more Frith prints from this book, possibly as gifts for friends and family, you can buy them at half price (with no additional postage and handling costs).

Have your Mounted Prints framed
For an extra £14.95 per print* you can have your mounted print(s) framed in an elegant polished wood and gilt moulding, overall size 16 x 13 inches (no additional postage and handling required).

*** IMPORTANT!**

These special prices are only available if you order at the same time as you order your free mounted print. You must use the ORIGINAL VOUCHER on this page (no copies permitted). We can only despatch to one address.

Send completed Voucher form to:
The Francis Frith Collection, Frith's Barn, Teffont, Salisbury, Wiltshire SP3 5QP

CHOOSE ANY IMAGE FROM THIS BOOK

Voucher *for* ***FREE*** *and Reduced Price Frith Prints*

Please do not photocopy this voucher. Only the original is valid, so please fill it in, cut it out and return it to us with your order.

Picture ref no	Page no	Qty	Mounted @ £7.49	Framed + £14.95	Total Cost
		1	Free of charge*	£	£
			£7.49	£	£
			£7.49	£	£
			£7.49	£	£
			£7.49	£	£
			£7.49	£	£
Please allow 28 days for delivery			* Post & handling (UK)		£2.25
			Total Order Cost		£

Title of this book . . . .
I enclose a cheque/postal order for £ . . . .
made payable to 'The Francis Frith Collection'

OR please debit my Mastercard / Visa / Switch / Amex card
(credit cards please on all overseas orders), details below

Card Number

Issue No (Switch only) Valid from (Amex/Switch)

Expires Signature

Name Mr/Mrs/Ms ....
Address ....
....
....
.... Postcode ....
Daytime Tel No ....
Email ....

Valid to 31/12/05

Free Print - see overleaf

Would you like to find out more about Francis Frith?

We have recently recruited some entertaining speakers who are happy to visit local groups, clubs and societies to give an illustrated talk documenting Frith's travels and photographs. If you are a member of such a group and are interested in hosting a presentation, we would love to hear from you.

Our speakers bring with them a small selection of our local town and county books, together with sample prints. They are happy to take orders. A small proportion of the order value is donated to the group who have hosted the presentation. The talks are therefore an excellent way of fundraising for small groups and societies.

Can you help us with information about any of the Frith photographs in this book?

We are gradually compiling an historical record for each of the photographs in the Frith archive. It is always fascinating to find out the names of the people shown in the pictures, as well as insights into the shops, buildings and other features depicted.

If you recognize anyone in the photographs in this book, or if you have information not already included in the author's caption, do let us know. We would love to hear from you, and will try to publish it in future books or articles.

Our production team

Frith books are produced by a small dedicated team at offices in the converted Grade II listed 18th-century barn at Teffont near Salisbury, illustrated above. Most have worked with the Frith Collection for many years. All have in common one quality: they have a passion for the Frith Collection. The team is constantly expanding, but currently includes:

Jason Buck, John Buck, Douglas Mitchell-Burns, Ruth Butler, Heather Crisp, Isobel Hall, Julian Hight, Peter Horne, James Kinnear, Karen Kinnear, Tina Leary, David Marsh, Sue Molloy, Kate Rotondetto, Dean Scource, Eliza Sackett, Terence Sackett, Sandra Sampson, Adrian Sanders, Sandra Sanger, Julia Skinner, Lewis Taylor, Shelley Tolcher and Lorraine Tuck.